Distributed Computing 4 Kids and Executives
By Holden Karau

Pigs Can Fly Labs mailing address:

9450 SW Gemini Dr, PMB 41687, Beaverton, OR 97008

For those interested in corporate or educational licensing or sales of Distributed Computing 4 Kids and Executives you can reach corporate sales at sales@pigscanfly.ca

Illustrations by: Johnny Kiotis
Formatting by: Annalise Cole & Toria Laughlin

Part I

Front Matter

This book is broken up into two parts. The first part introduces the concept of distributed systems using garden gnomes, and the second part looks at how these concepts translate into code.

Acknowledgments

Like all books I've been involved in writing, and like almost everyone I've heard about, this book took much longer than expected. I'd like to thank the wonderful PyData community for listening to early versions of this as a talk, the ASF Spark community for letting me explore new strange ideas, and most of all my wife and partners for listening to the hundreds of ideas I've had about what I want to do. This book would not have been possible without contributions from Timo Aho, Yaara and Itai Yaffe.

Who is This Books For?

There are computer programs everywhere. You use programs, or apps, on your mobile phone when you message your friends, check the weather, or play games. Executives often use apps for less exciting things too like expense reports and calendars (or their assistant does for them). This book is for kids interested in learning how to make computer programs that run across multiple computers and executives trying to understand how to solve bigger problems. This process is needed for problems that are too big or slow to be handled on one computer.

There are many problems like this. Recommending exciting videos, like Netflix or YouTube, need data about who watched videos and liked them. Building a search engine (like Google) involves visiting every web page. This way, when you ask Google to find something, it can look at everything. If we tried either of these projects on one computer, it would take a long time. Instead, we split the work up on many computers.

Most kinds of work can be shared. Trying to organize all the clothes in a store involves many people working together. Just like with computers, some work is easier on your own. For example, you may want to organize your room, desk, or favourite items. Explaining where you want everything to go could take too long. Knowing when to get help on a problem and knowing when to use multiple computers are both difficult.

When we use multiple computers to solve a problem, it's often called "distributed computing." Several tools allow you to make distributed programs. Yes, you guessed right; distributed programs achieve distributed computing. Think of the term "distributed" as "spread across," and in our case, it is programs spread across multiple computers.

Computers do not understand our languages. Thus, we need to use a special computer language called code. With the computer language, we describe what the programs do. There are so many tools available to help us distribute our programs. Oops, my bad. "Programs" here means text, or pieces of code, that computers understand.

Large Language Models (often called LLMs), like ChatGPT and Claude, use a special kind of math to somewhat understand our language, but even when you ask ChatGPT the same question it may provide a different answer. You can use LLMs to help you create code or understand what's wrong with your code. Sometimes LLMs are "just" called AI, but there are many different types of AI beyond LLMs.

The book is broken into two parts. The first part introduces the general concepts of a distributed system like Spark. The second part builds on top of the first and shows how to use the concepts from the first to build a program.

There are many tools, and we can't cover all of them here. Instead, this book will focus on getting you started with one of these tools, called Apache Spark. Spark is a very complex tool, so we only cover the basics. If this book is popular, I may do a follow up for some other tools I like (like Dask, Ray, or Daft).

WILL WORK FOR TEA
TEA

I think everything is easier to understand with examples, so we have one in this book. The example in this book centers around finding popular tags on Instagram. You may have heard about Instagram: it is an application used for sharing photos and videos. To share pictures, you need an account; however, you do not need one for this book. If your friends are on Instagram, that's great. If not, just find some accounts that share photos you like. You can also skip the latter exercises if you want.

The Start of an Adventure

Alex and her friend Ziva play most weekends. This weekend, they want to take photos for Instagram. They want their photos to be of a topic that is popular with their friends. To know what is popular, they want to see the recent top tags used by their many friends. The Instagram app doesn't show what is trending with just their friends. So they decide to try and figure this out.

Looking up the top tags for each of their friends, one at a time, would take far too long, as Alex and Ziva have many friends. Think superstars like Ariana Grande or JoJo Siwa level friends. They would also need to add up the results and sort them. So Alex and Ziva ask some of their friends, the four garden gnomes, to help them.

Garden gnomes normally don't spend a lot of time on Instagram. Instead, they are on Instagnome. But these garden gnomes love working together on projects almost as much as they love tea. They like tea a lot because it can get chilly outside.

Our Garden Gnome Friends Offer to Help

In exchange for some tea, the gnomes agree to help Alex and Ziva. The gnomes will look up the tags from recent posts of Alex and Ziva's friends. Ziva asks all of the gnomes to install Instagram on their phones.

The gnomes start by downloading Instagram. While it installs, Alex and Ziva write down a list of their friends' Instagram accounts. They use a stack of index cards so the list can easily be split up and divided among the gnomes. Splitting up a single page of paper would be difficult to get right.

TEA

Getting to Work

The gnomes talk to decide who should be the leader for this project. A leader is needed so that they can make choices quickly. They agree that the gnome with the blue hat should be the leader.

She looks at the stack of cards to guess how many each gnome should take so that it is equal. If the gnomes don't get a fair share, then those with fewer cards will finish before the others. It takes a gnome a minute to handle one card. If one gnome takes 30 cards and another gnome 60 cards, the first gnome would have to wait another half hour for her friend to finish. The gnome with fewer cards would also get bored and drink all the tea.

Each gnome, except for the leader, grabs a share of the cards. The leader is busy keeping track of the work. Once each of them has Instagram installed and gets their share of cards, they start looking up each account. When they load the account, they check below the most recent photo to see the tags and write down each tag on a new card. So, if underneath the photo it said, "Morning with the #bestdog #coffee," the gnome would write down "#bestdog" and "#coffee." It would look something like the cards to the left.

Once done, each gnome will have a card for each different tag in the profiles that the gnome saw. Each card will have the number of times the tag appeared in the profiles on that gnome's list.

#CUTE
#FASHION
#VIRAL
#SATURDAY
#TRAVEL
#CAT
#PUFFIN

ZZZZ

One of the Gnomes Got Tired

Just like when playing a game or doing a group project, sometimes someone has to leave. The gnome in the red hat was tired from being up late reading. Partway through trying to sort his cards, he fell asleep. The leader asked the gnome in the green hat to take over for him. Ze agrees and picks up the cards and finishes the work.

Combining the Counts

The hot water for their tea starts to boil, adding a sense of urgency to the project.

The leader (in the blue hat) thinks: How can we make sure we have the counts of the same tags together? If the gnome with the red hat had a picture with the tag #bestdog, and the purple hat gnome did too, neither would have the full count. Each gnome would think that #bestdog was only used once, when it was actually used twice.

The leader decides that the best way to solve this is to assign gnomes certain words. To decide who is responsible for which tag, they use the first letter of each tag to decide who it belongs to. She decides to make the first gnome responsible for the letters a to g, the second for h to k, and so on. They'll need to trade cards, which will take a little time. However by trading, any duplicate tags will be together with the same gnome. Each gnome goes and delivers their index cards with the tallies/counts of the words to their friend's toadstools.

After completing the trading, they can start combining the cards. When they find a card with a new tag,they don't need to do anything special. When they find an index card with a tag they've seen before, they add up count of all the cards with those tags.

PUFFIN

Finishing Up with the Gnomes

Now, each gnome has index cards with different tags and their counts. They each go through their list of tags and find the one with the highest count. Each gnome gives the lead gnome the index card with the highest count. The lead gnome gets the index card with the highest count from the other gnomes and tells Alex and Ziva what it is. Since #puffinlife is the most popular tag, they set about taking some photos with their puffin friend.

N TO Z
H TO M
ZZZ
A TO G

Taking Some Photos

They balance the puffin on top of one of the toadstools and take pictures wearing silly hats. Their stuffed animal friend, Puffy, hears them talking about puffins and comes down to join in the fun. Puffy is genderqueer and uses they/them pronouns. Puffy takes a photo with Alex, Ziva, and their Puffin friend. They, of course, tag it with #puffinlife for their friends to see.

Going Beyond the Most Recent Photo

The gnomes go off to sleep, as the herbal tea has made them tired. One of Alex's moms, Holden, stops by to see how the Instagram shoot is going. Alex and Ziva tell her what they did with the gnomes. Holden says it sounds very similar to what she does at work.

Alex and Ziva ask her if they could use computers to find popular tags. Holden says that yes, this can be done with computers. A computer wouldn't fall asleep because it was out late, and it can look at more photos than the gnomes. With a tool called Apache Spark, which Holden works on, Alex and Ziva could spread the work across many computers.

The next part in this book will look at how the techniques with the garden gnomes are used with computers.

Part II

Front matter

This is an optional bonus to part 1 where we turn the concepts into code. By now you already understand how distributed systems work, so if that's what you are going for this is a perfectly ok place to stop.

We build on the concepts from Part 1 and turn the concepts into a program. Following the exercises in this book will be easier with a traditional computer. You do not need to do the exercises, you can also just read and think about them. Some online Spark notebooks can be accessed from tablets and phones, although the interface often isn't well designed.

For kids, as they progress through this book, they will reach points where it is strongly suggested that they receive additional help. The helper can be a parent or guardian, but it could also be a librarian, teacher, or sibling. For executives, your Data Science group or IT should have the right folks. They don't need to know Apache Spark, but it will help if they have some programming experience. Someone with experience working with computers (or someone with time and interest) is best.

For executives the helper can be a data scientist, engineer, or an intern who's handy with computers.

You can also choose to have AI help you with the exercises when you get stuck.

Setting up and getting access to the tools is where additional help can be useful. Some optional online tools need an adult (or in companies IT/legal department) to agree to use them. Some of them can also cost money. Even free tools without agreements can be complicated to set up.

There is a companion notebook with a solution at https://github.com/holdenk/distributedcomputing4kids/blob/master/code/Sample%20Solution.ipynb . There are also solutions to some of the extra exercises in the same directory.

Some important terms related to computers

As mentioned earlier, programming languages give us a way to tell the computer what we want it to do. Python is the name of the one which we will use in this book. There are many other programming languages with different strengths. Some others that the author has worked with include C++, R, Python, Java, Scala, Julia, and Clojure. Programming languages can have interesting names. Programmers like to have fun with names. The author chose Python for a few reasons, besides the cool name.

Python is often used for working with knowledge that is understood by computers: data. What is data? When we work with Instagram, in our example, we consider photos, captions, and tags as data. Similarly, when working with the entire internet, we would consider web pages to be data. A list of the names of your friends could also be data.

Python is used in schools and companies, from Amazon to Google, which means your skills can be used in the real world. You can check with your school for any course about Python. If your school doesn't have any, there are many online courses too.

There are lots of great videos and books about Python for everyone. If you wish to learn Python first, Python for Kids by Jason R. Briggs can be a good book. The Hour of Python website can also help and has lots of examples. If you like learning from videos, there are many amazing Python videos on YouTube.

If you get stuck on any programming concept you may benefit by looking at another resource. You can also try searching on Google.com, or asking someone for help. If they get stuck, too, they can check out websites like stackoverflow.com/questions. Sometimes, people are not nice on that website, so having an someone to help you is good.

Hopefully you are excited to jump in. Let's get back to Apache Spark, as promised. Generally, a program can run on one computer. However, since this book is focused on distributed computing, we will use multiple computers. How? Apache Spark to the rescue! Spark is a tool to help multiple computers work together on the same problem. This is only one type of distributed computing. We will talk about some other types at the end of this book.

Spark, the tool, and Python, the programming language, are together called PySpark. Spark works in more programming languages than just Python. When Spark is used with the R programming language, it is sometimes called SparkR. Spark also works in Scala, but since it started there, it doesn't have a special name.

When we have a group of computers working together, we call this a cluster. Spark can simulate a cluster, letting us start with just one computer. We'll discuss this more when we start using Spark.

Getting Started with the Computer

For this part of the book you may need to understand Python. If you don't know much about Python yet, don't worry! There are many great resources and programs to help you learn; these are covered in the previous section. Alex and Ziva will be waiting for you when you get back! (We do cover Python as we go, but it is not our focus.)

You will want to get someone to help you access a Spark and Python notebook. Installing Spark has many steps. There are instructions at http://www.distributedcomputing4kids.com/local_setup/ . You'll want to get someone to help you with this. It can be quite complex, so tell your helper not to feel bad if they get stuck.

We'll start by having Spark simulate a cluster; this is called local mode. Spark will run copies of itself many times to pretend it is on different computers. Local mode is good enough that many Spark programmers use it to test their work. While a real cluster gives us more power, we can wait to use one until we know our program works. This helps since real clusters can cost additional money.

Our next steps

The first thing we will do is write some Python code to help us look up the most popular tags for one person's Instagram feed. We'll start by doing this with one specific person so we can see if it is working.

Once we have figured out how to look up the tags for one person's Instagram, we need to make this work for anyone. This can be done by creating something called a function. You might use functions in math class already, or executives might see them in spreadsheets. In computers, when we talk about a function we mean a bit of code that can be used by another piece of code. We'll talk more about computer functions when we make our first function. We will make a function that will take an input (sometimes called a parameter), which tells the function whose tags to look up.

In addition to the functions we will make, Python has many built-in functions. These are functions provided to us by Python. We'll see some of them soon, including `print` and `map`.

When you want a function to do something not already in Python, you can see if anyone has shared a function they made. The PyPi website is a great place to find shared functions and tools. One of the great things about Python is that many people share some of what they build with it.

While we have code samples in this book, you should download the exercise notebook from https://github.com/holdenk/distributedcomputing4kids/blob/master/code. There is also a solutions notebook there. If you get stuck, feel free to take a look at the solutions. I do this all the time while they are learning.

Importing the Library

New computer programs are often built using other programs. It's like how, when writing, you don't need to make your own paper. One thing we need to do is teach the computer how to understand Instagram's website.

Thankfully, some other people were interested in solving that problem and published a program for understanding Instagram called instagram-scraper. The instagram-scraper tool is very powerful, but it isn't designed to be used by another program. To make things easier, Holden put the instagram-scraper inside of a library called basic_instagram_library. In computing, libraries are collections of software designed for use by other software instead of humans. They have that name since libraries are powerful collections of knowledge and tools.

Some libraries are built into Python, but since basic_instagram_library doesn't come with Python, we need to install the library. This is similar to having the gnomes install Instagram on their phones. For your local computer in your notebook, the following command installs the

```
!pip install basic_instagram_library
```

basic_instagram_library:
The "!" at the start of the command tells the notebook to run a program. The program "pip" is a tool for installing Python libraries, so we can ask pip to install our library.

In a notebook, once you want to run what you have written, press the “shift” and “enter” keys at the same time. If you don't do this, the notebook will assume you want to keep writing more instructions.

To tell the computer that we want to use a library, we type `import name_of_library`. The library we are using is basic_instagram_library. So we import it as:

```
import basic_instagram_library
```

This is Python, so we don't need to put a "!" at the front of the code.

If this fails, ask whoever is helping you to ensure that the Instagram library was properly installed. They can double check the instructions from the previous page.

Normally when we import a library we have to type out the library name each time we use a part of it. Sometimes, we only want specific parts of a library. To import just one piece, we type `from name_of_library import part_i_want`. Then when we use `part_i_want`, we can just type it as such instead of `name_of_library.part_i_want`. This can be easier to access the parts we want.

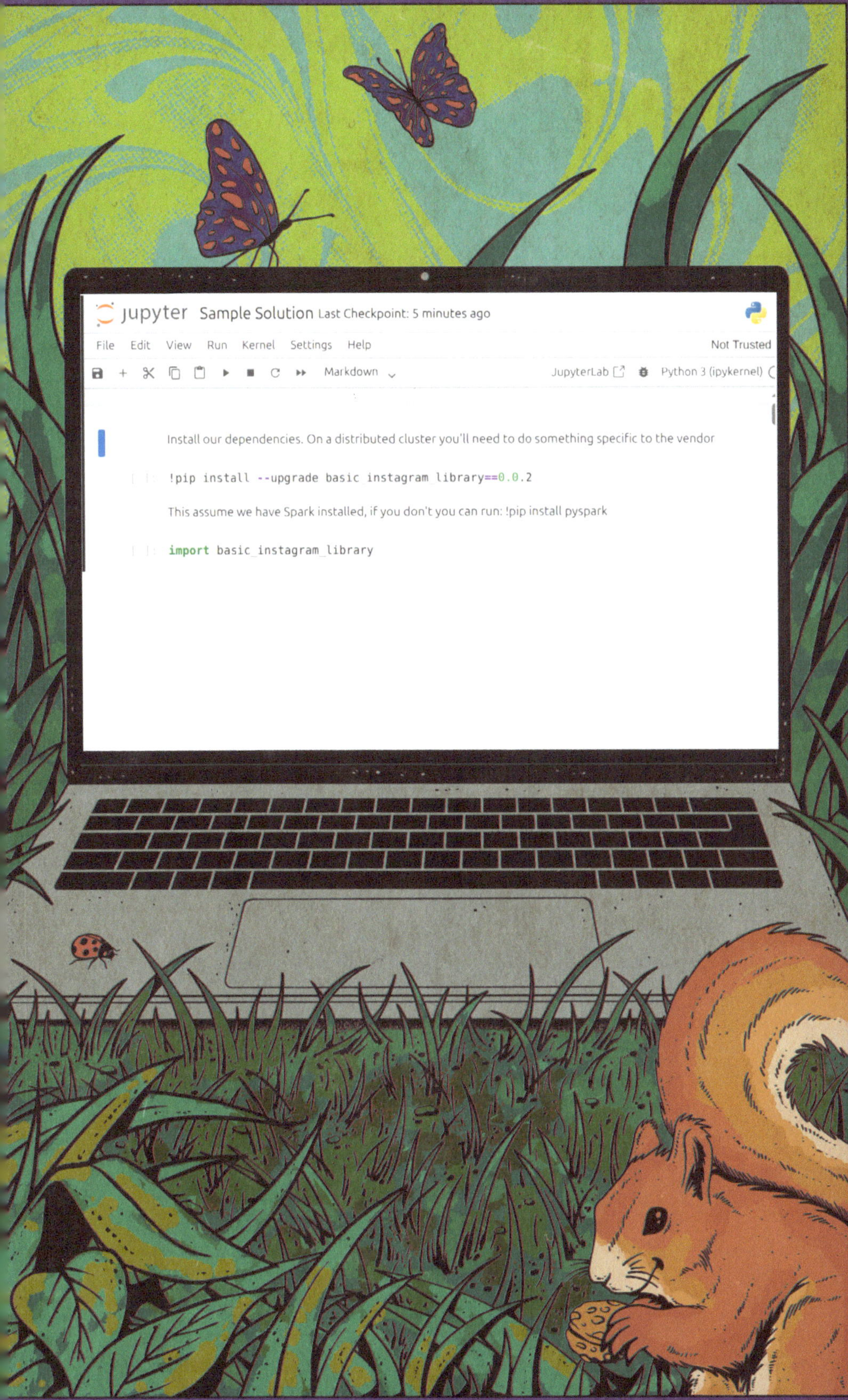
jupyter Sample Solution Last Checkpoint: 5 minutes ago
File Edit View Run Kernel Settings Help
Not Trusted
Markdown
JupyterLab
Python 3 (ipykernel)
Install our dependencies. On a distributed cluster you'll need to do something specific to the vendor
!pip install --upgrade basic_instagram_library==0.0.2
This assume we have Spark installed, if you don't you can run: !pip install pyspark
import basic_instagram_library

Giving Things Names (Variables)

The first thing to do is pick a friend's Instagram page to test with. Alex and Ziva decided to start with their friend "nanook_of_the_burgh" (a fuzzy dog). Once we've decided who we want to test with, we can try and find the tags in their posts.

One important concept for computers is variables. Variables allow us to give things names. Then instead of typing or computing the same thing many times, we can use a variable. This is useful when something takes a long time to compute. This way we can avoid waiting a long time. Another time is if we are typing the same thing. This gives us less typing, and if we need to change it we only need to change the variable definition. For example, we could store the name of our friend like so:

```
friend_name = "nanook_of_the_burgh"
```

Let's talk a bit about the quotation marks. They aren't because someone else said the phrase first. The quotes tell Python that "nanook_of_the_burgh" is not code or a command to execute but a string. A string is made up of characters/letters and can be many words, one word, or even the empty string"". Now, if we ever need our friend's name again we can use the friend_name variable.

Variables can also help others read and understand your software.

Exercise: Make a variable with the name of an Instagram account.
Exercise Part 2: Make a variable called food with what you ate for breakfast. We'll use it later.

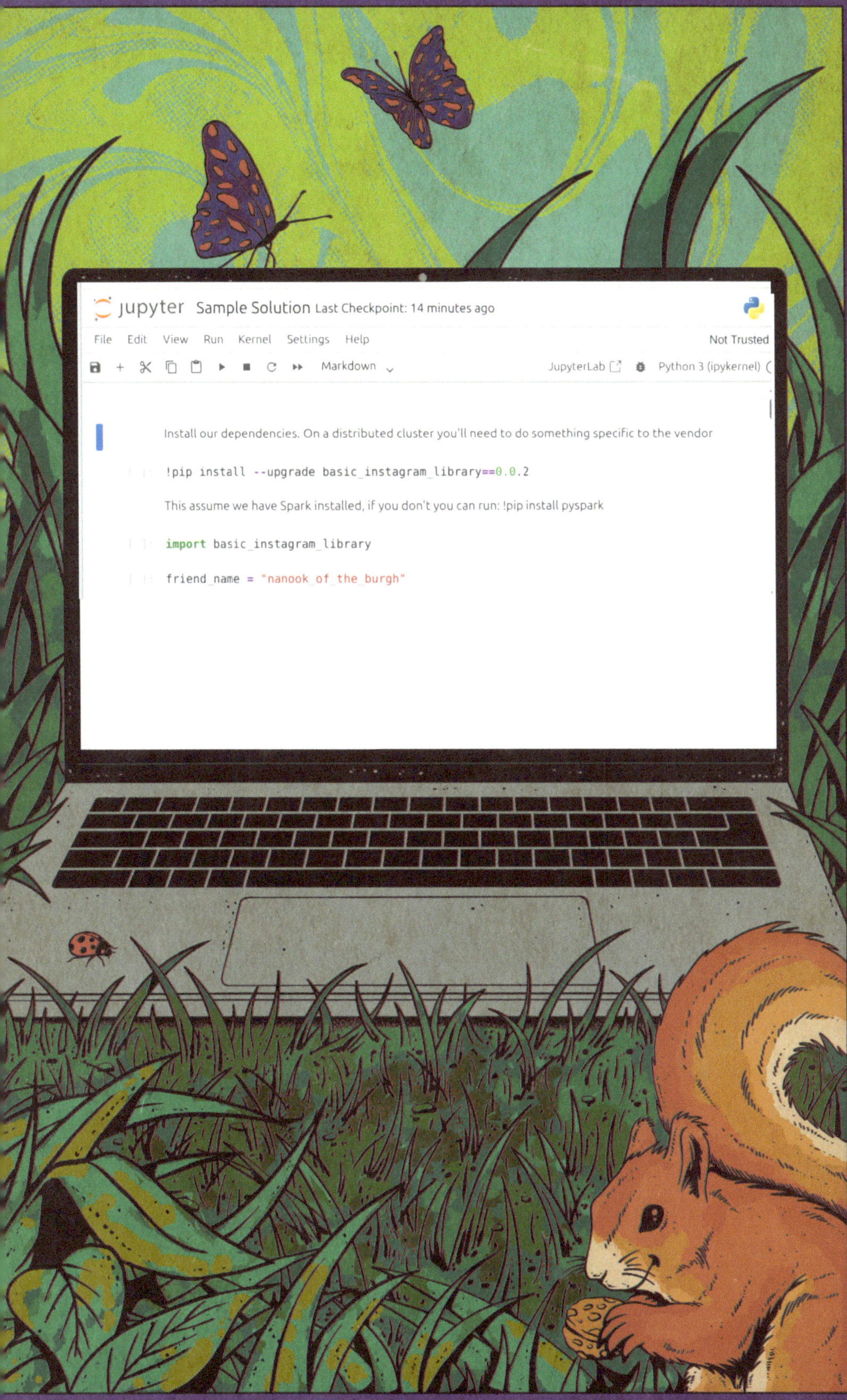
jupyter
Sample Solution
Last Checkpoint: 14 minutes ago
File
Edit
View
Run
Kernel
Settings
Help
Not Trusted
Markdown
JupyterLab
Python 3 (ipykernel)
Install our dependencies. On a distributed cluster you'll need to do something specific to the vendor
!pip install --upgrade basic_instagram_library==0.0.2
This assume we have Spark installed, if you don't you can run: !pip install pyspark
import basic_instagram_library
friend_name = "nanook_of_the_burgh"

Looking Up Our Friend's Instagram Page and Finding the Tags

The basic_instagram_library has documentation on how to use it at https://github.com/holdenk/distributedcomputing4kids/tree/master/code/basic_instagram_library. The function we need to use is called "find_words", which gives us all of the words used in a person's post. Since the function comes from a library, we type "library.function" so Python can find the right one.

```
basic_instagram_library.find_words(
  "nanook_of_the_burgh")
```

Exercise: Use the friend_name variable instead of typing out the Instagram handle. The result should be the same unless Nanook posted a new photo.

When you run this function you should see words from nanook_of_the_burgh's posts. These are the words, including tags, underneath the photos on Instagram. However, we just want to look at tags. Tags start with "#", so we need to filter our results.

Looking up the words can take time, so we want to store them inside our computer. We can save the result of the function call in a variable.

```
words=basic_instagram_library.find_words(
  "nanook_of_the_burgh")
```

We could simplify this and use the variable name we gave for our friend:

```
words=basic_instagram_library.find_words(
  friend_name)
```

A really useful function in Python is called print. We can use it to see variables. For example, we can see what is inside of the words variable:

```
print(words)
```

This results in something like:

"[...]"

The brackets [ ] in what is printed tell us that we are printing a list. Looking at each element, we can see that we have a list of words.

Notebooks also display the last part of the command, so you can just type `words` and see the output.

```
words
```

Sometimes we want to get a specific element in the list. We can get the first element of the list by typing `results[0]`. This can be confusing, since the first element of a list is accessed with a 0 rather than 1, which is how many people begin their lists. Starting counting lists at 0 is common in many programming languages and is called "zero-indexing." We can get other elements in the list in the same way by using different numbers . We can print out the second word from the list by using `print` and `[]` together.

```
print(words[1])
```

Exercise: Get the fifth word from our list of words and print it out.
Exercise Part 2: What happens when you try and get a word beyond those we got? The len function will tell you how many elements are in a list.

If we look at the words returned by the function, we can see some words aren't tags. We'll need to figure out a way to restrict the words to just those starting with "#". In order to do this, let's look at making functions.

jupyter Sample Solution Last Checkpoint: 17 minutes ago
File Edit View Run Kernel Settings Help
Not Trusted
Markdown
JupyterLab
Python 3 (ipykernel)
Introducing Functions
# Function of what I sometimes thinks cats say
def cat(param):
return "no."
cat("Come here please")
def cat(param):
return "no." # TODO: translate to cat
cat("Come here please")
def isTag(word):
return word.startswith("#")
tags_iter = filter(isTag, words)
tags = list(tags_iter)
tags

Making a Function

Code tells the computer what we want it to do. Telling it to do the same thing with small changes over and over can be boring. A function is a reusable piece of code. Some functions take inputs (sometimes called parameters), which allows us to make small changes. If you've ever played mad-libs or put your email in a form, you can think of inputs in a similar way. Except we can look up what the words are for. For us, we can change who the function is looking up the words for, without having to write the code again. Some functions produce a result (a process called returning). For example, a programmer developed a function that counts and returns the number of likes and shares of your Insta post. Some functions do things on the computer, like how print shows us information, called side-effects.

Some cats seem to ignore almost everything. The first function we make will take an input, ignore it, and return the word "no", so we call the function "cat":

```
def cat(param):
   return "no."
```

Using a function is known as calling. We can test this function by pretending we are calling a cat: `cat("Come here please")` and see it return the word "no."

Python cares about spaces! This means that if we wrote the function above without spaces before the word "return", would not work:

```
def cat(param):
return "no."
```

Python uses the number of spaces on a line to determine if we're still writing inside of the function or if we've finished. This is different from many other programming languages, which use curly brackets { } instead.

Exercise: Make a dog function that prints out bark and returns yes.

The number sign "#" also has a special meaning in Python. Sometimes when you are writing code you will want to leave yourself a note. You can tell the computer that you're leaving a note for humans rather than the computer by adding a "#" mark like this:

```
def cat(param):
   return "no." # TODO: translate to cat. Is this "meow"?
```

This is called a comment. Comments are useful because we often don't remember what we were doing before when we are writing code. Also some programs are built by multiple people working together, so comments can help with collaboration.

Exercise: Add a comment to your dog function.

Making Choices

If our programs always did the same thing, that wouldn't be very exciting. So, we can ask the computer to do something only if something is true. For example, we can ask the computer to print out "farts" if we tell it we ate beans. We can use "==" to ask the computer if two things are the same. You might wonder why there isn't just one equal sign or "=". Since we use "=" to assign values, we need a different way to check if things are equal.

```
# Print out farts if we ate beans
if food == "beans":
   print("farts")
```

Exercise: Try setting the variable food to "beans" and running the above example.

Exercise Part 2: You can change the contents/value of a variable in the same way we set them. Change the value of food to "Beans" and run our example again. When does the computer fart?

As before, Python cares about spaces! Here we use the spaces to tell Python we are writing inside the if statement.

This is an if statement. In addition to if, there is also elif (short for else if) and else. You can use these as part of an if statement to make complex decisions. Here we can go beyond beans and also consider candy.

```
if food == "beans":
    print("farts")
elif food == "candy":
    print("HI! Can I have more candy?")
else:
   print("Can I have candy or beans?")
```

While cats might ignore what we try to tell them, dogs probably won't. So, if we tell a dog to "walk," it might bark twice. We can use an if statement to change what we do based on what is passed to us.

Exercise: Make a dog function that prints out "bark bark" if we give the function walk as an input; otherwise, print bark once. Note: there is more than one way to do this.

Exercise: Make your cat function better by ignoring everything except for food.

Checking What Letter a String Starts With...

To get just the words that begin with a "#", we need something a bit more useful. We will write a function that takes in a string and then tells us if that string starts with a "#".

To do this, we'll use a built-in function on strings called `startswith`. As the name suggests, we can use this to check what a string starts with. The startswith function is built into Python, but in a library. We can access it through the built-in "str" library.

```
def is_tag(word):
   return str.startswith(word, "#")
```

Bonus Exercise: We can also use a string as if it was a list of letters. So if you want to see the third letter in the variable food you could write `food[2]`. What this returns depends on what the value of food is. If it was "beans" it would return "a". Use this to write a version of is_tag that doesn't use startswith. Extra bonus: use the len function to so your new function handles the empty string (e.g. "").

Alternate Bonus Exercise:
`startswith` is a little different than the functions we are making today because it is also defined on strings. This does sound weird, but stay with this. There are many different strings, like "i like coffee" and "cheese". All of these strings are part of a class called String. `startswith` is called a "member function" because it is a member of a class (namely String). When using a member function instead of just writing

`startswith(param)` we take the string we want to check and add `.startswith(param)` to the end of the name of the string. Rewrite is_tag to use startswith as a member function.

jupyter Sample Solution Last Checkpoint: 18 minutes ago
File Edit View Run Kernel Settings Help
Not Trusted
Markdown
JupyterLab
Python 3 (ipykernel)
[ ]: def get_tags(username):
import basic_instagram_library
words = basic_instagram_library.find_words(username)
def isTag(word):
return word.startswith("#")
tags_iter = filter(isTag, words)
return list(tags_iter)
[ ]: get_tags("hkarau")
[ ]: get_tags("nanook_of_the_burgh")
[ ]: awesome_people = ["hkarau", "rovetastic"]
[ ]: awesome_tags_iter = map(get_tags, awesome_people)
awesome_tags = list(awesome_tags_iter)
[ ]: awesome_tags
Getting started with Spark
[ ]: from pyspark import *

Making Our Tag Lookup Into a Function

We've got the tags for a specific user, but it took a lot of typing. Now we want to turn our previous code into a function to use it for all of our friends. To do this, we take what we've written in and put it inside of a function definition. Since we want this to work for anyone, not just Nanook, we use a parameter called `username` in place of his name.

```
def get_tags(username):
    import basic_instagram_library
words=basic_instagram_library.find_words(username)
    def is_tag(word):
        return word.startswith("#")
    tags_iter = filter(is_tag, words)
    return list(tags_iter)
```

We can verify that this works by calling our function with "nanook_of_the_burgh" and checking if the output is the same.

```
get_tags("nanook_of_the_burgh")
```

While we are here, we can talk about "scoping." Our program is fairly small, so if all of the functions and variables we wrote were always visible in our code, it would be ok. However, most programs are much bigger. So when we are inside of a function, the new functions or variables we define are visible only inside that function. Normally we'd get an error if we tried to use is_tag outside of get_tags. However, we already made one that wasn't inside of get_tags.

Applying our Function to a List

To write a list in Python you put the elements in between brackets [ ] and put commas between each element. You might notice that this is similar to how lists are printed out. We can start by making a list of Holden and Timbit's Instagram handles.

```
["hkarau", "fluffylittletimbit"]
```

To make this list usable elsewhere, we can give it a name: "awesome_people."

```
awesome_people=["hkarau", "fluffylittletimbit"]
```

A common thing to do is to apply a function to the elements in a list. We used `filter` to do this previously. Python's `map` function also applies a function to the elements in the list. `map` creates an iterator with the result of the provided function.

As with `filter` returning an iterator, we might want to use our tags more than once. We can convert the iterator into a list by using the `list` function as before.

Using `map` and `list`, we can run our lookup_tags function on awesome_people:

```
awesome_tags_iter = map(get_tags, awesome_people)
awesome_tags = list(awesome_tags_iter)
```

Exercise: There are probably several people you think are awesome on Instagram. Make a list called my_friends with your friends and run the previous example on it. What do you get?

If you have a lot of friends, this may run slowly, as it looks up the tags for each user, one at a time. Instead, we can run this lookup on different parts of the list at the same time (often called parallel processing).

We don't always need to use multiple computers to do parallel processing. Computers can run multiple copies of the same software. When we use multiple computers it's called "distributed computing." This can be even faster because a single computer can only do so much work.

jupyter Sample Solution Last Checkpoint: 19 minutes ago
File Edit View Run Kernel Settings Help
Not Trusted
Markdown
JupyterLab
Python 3 (ipykernel)
Getting started with Spark
[ ]: from pyspark import *
from pyspark.sql import *
[ ]: spark_session = SparkSession.builder.getOrCreate()
sc = spark_session.sparkContext
[ ]: awesome_people_rdd = sc.parallelize(awesome_people)
[ ]: awesome_tags_rdd = awesome_people_rdd.map(get_tags)
[ ]: flat_awesome_tags_rdd = awesome_people_rdd.flatMap(get_tags)
[ ]: flat_awesome_tags_rdd.first()
[ ]: def word_pair(word):
return (word, 1)
[ ]: tag_pairs_rdd = flat_awesome_tags_rdd.map(word_pair)
[ ]: def sum_count(count1, count2):

Getting Started with Spark, or Starting our Distributed System

The first step to working with Spark is importing some important parts of the Spark library. Spark is complex, so it's broken up into different parts, because not all programs need to use all of its capabilities. As with the previous code these imports go into the notebook.

```
from pyspark import *
from pyspark.sql import *
```

The "from x import *" is a bit different from what we did before. It lets us reference things in pyspark without having to type `pyspark.thing` or knowing all of the things we are importing. This can be a problem if something we import has the name of one of our own things.

Now that we have Spark's libraries imported we can make the SparkContext. A SparkContext lets us talk to our cluster.

```
spark_session=SparkSession.builder.getOrCreate()
sc=spark_session.sparkContext
```

If you're in the cloud, you may find that there is already a SparkContext in your notebook. This is because some programs are only built for use with Spark, so they start it for you. Thankfully, with the `getOrCreate` function, Spark will just reuse the existing SparkContext.

You may see that we've written a variable using words with _s between them, like "spark_session." This style is snake_case, and is common with Python programmers. Another style is capital letters to start each new word; this is called camelCase. camelCase is common with Java and Scala, in which Spark is built. These styles exist because we can't have spaces in our variable names. This can be confusing, but either style is fine.

Making a Distributed Collection (Resilient Distributed Dataset)

To do our work on many computers, we need our data on many computers. Spark can take our list and split it up. Spark can then put different pieces of the list on different computers. In Spark this function is called `parallelize`. It takes a local list and turns it into a distributed collection. Spark's distributed collections are called Resilient Distributed Datasets (RDDs) so we'll call our example `awesome_people_rdd`.

```
awesome_people_rdd=sc.parallelize(awesome_people)
```

Now, awesome_people_rdd is a distributed collection. This allows us to work on multiple computers.

Exercise: Do this with your list of friends on Instagram, too.

Note: You don't have to call this awesome_people_rdd; you can pick another name you like better. Just try and pick a name that will help you remember what it is for tomorrow.

Spark has other methods to make a distributed collection. If the data is too big to fit on a single computer, it's often stored in many different computers from the start. There are different approaches to this, and Spark can understand most of them. Another way to make a distributed collection is to make one based on an existing collection. This is the most common way to make a distributed collection, and we'll look at one way how to do this next.

Applying a Parallel/Distributed Function

We can now use `map` on our distributed collection. This is similar to how we used the map function on a local collection. There are some important differences, though. The `map` function we used earlier is defined by Python and works on local collections. Spark defines its own map function, but because these functions only work on Spark's distributed data, they are accessed differently. Instead of writing `map(function_name, list_name)` we write `rdd_name.map(function_name)`.

```
awesome_tags_rdd=awesome_people_rdd.map(
  get_tags)
```

Spark has several other functions. Functions that return another RDD, like map, are often called transformations. A brief table that lists some common functions can be found in Appendix A. There is a complete list online as well.

We're interested in the counts for everyone together rather than separately for each person. Because `get_tags` returns a list, after using `map` on our RDD we have an RDD of lists. It will make our life easier to just have an RDD of the tags. Turning a list of lists into a flat list is called flattening. Spark has a built-in function called `flatMap` that flattens as it maps. We can use it as so:

```
flat_awesome_tags_rdd=awesome_people_rdd.flatMap(
  get_tags)
```

Peeking at the Results

Spark only does work when it becomes necessary. This is called "lazy evaluation." Spark keeps track of the work we ask it to do. So when we ask it to look up the tags, rather than looking them up right away, it makes a note of what we asked.

Later, when we save the results or look at them, Spark will finally do what we've asked it to do.

To make sure we did not make a mistake making `flat_awesome_tags_rdd`, we can call the function `first`. Spark will then show us one of the results. This forces Spark to figure out how to make flat_awesome_tags_rdd. With lazy evaluation mistakes can otherwise be hidden.

```
flat_awesome_tags_rdd.first()
```

Note: You might wonder why we can't write `flat_awesome_tags_rdd[0]`. In a local collection doing that would give us the first element. However, because `flat_awesome_tags_rdd` is a distributed collection accessing elements involves talking to other computers. This is slower than accessing elements on a single computer. To remind people of this Spark, uses different names.

Starting the Count

Now that we have the tags, we want to get ready to count them. To start with, we can pair each tag with the number one. The number one represents that the tag has been seen once. If we've seen the same word multiple times, don't worry; we'll combine the pairs in the next section.

To accomplish this, we'll write a function. When we want to store two things together, like our tag and number, we can use a tuple. A tuple is similar to a list but you can't change its contents. Sometimes people call tuples of two a key-value pair, with the first thing being the key and the second thing being the value. This is like writing two things on one index card.

```
def word_pair(word):
   return (word, 1)
```

Now that we have the function, we'll use `map` again to make a new RDD.

```
tag_pairs = flat_awesome_tags_rdd.map(word_pair)
```

If we were to peek at the `tag_pairs` RDD, we would see a tuple of the tag and the number one.

Combing the Results

Similar to the gnomes' index cards, the tags are spread out on different computers. We can ask Spark to combine the counts for each of the keys that are the same. To do this, we write a function that Spark will run whenever it finds two tags that are the same.

```
def sum_count(count1, count2):
    return count1 + count2
```

We can then ask Spark to use our `sum_count` function to combine the results with the same key. The Spark function used to do this is called `reduceByKey`.

```
tag_counts_rdd=tag_pairs_rdd.reduceByKey(
    sum_count)
```

First, each computer checks to see if they have any of the same tags and adds the counts up. By doing this first, the number of pairs they have to transfer can be reduced. This is called optimization, as it can make things faster but is not required.

Then the primary computer gives the other computers responsibilities for different sets of tags. This is similar to how the lead gnome assigned letter ranges. The computers check for tags that belong to another computer and transfer them.

Once the transfer is finished, the computers check the pairs they got for the same tags and add the counts up.

This process is very similar to the one the gnomes used. Instead of index cards, we have tuples, and as transferring data between computers can be slow we have an optimization.

Sorting and Collecting the Results

If we don't have too many words, we can take our distributed collection and bring the result back as a local list we can look at. In addition to the `first` function, Spark has a `collect` function, which brings the contents of the rdd back as a list.

```
tag_counts_rdd.collect()
```

Sometimes, though, we have too much data to fit it all on one computer. Like if you tried to store all of Instagram on your phone. In those cases, we save the data in many files on different computers. For our project, though, we just want to see the most popular tags. So we sort the RDD and ask Spark to return a limited number of elements.

Spark's RDDs' have a `sortByKey` function, which will sort our RDD for us. However, by default, this function sorts on the key (in this case the tag) and in ascending order (low to high). Thankfully, we can change this by providing some inputs. To switch the result from ascending to descending we set the `ascending=False` parameter. To sort the RDD by count (value) instead of tags, we need to provide another function. Spark then applies our function and sorts using the result of it.

```
def get_cound(t):
   return t[1]
top_tags_rdd=tag_counts_rdd.sortByKey(
   ascending=False, keyfunc=get_count)
```

This may be the first time you've seen named parameters. So far we've used functions inputs by order. When there are many parameters this can get confusing.

To get just some of the elements Spark has a function called `take` which lets us specify how many results we want.

```
top_tags_rdd.take(5)
```

Taking Out the "Bad" Words

If you're going to show your new creation to a friend, teacher, or co-worker (for executives), the most popular tags might change between now and when you show them. This can be embarrassing if the words are mean or swear words. This has happened with very important presentations in front of thousands of people. If you can come up with a list of possible bad hashtags, then you can make sure they don't show up by using `filter`.

Exercise Part 1: Come up with a list of bad hashtags to take out of your results.
Exercise Part 2: Write a function that returns if a hashtag is bad.
Exercise Part 3: Use filter to apply this function to your `top_tags_rdd`.
Bonus 1: Convert the tags to lowercase.
Bonus 2: Lookup how Spark broadcast variables work and speed up the code.
Bonus 3: Lookup bloom filters to make this even faster.
Bonus 4: There is a new technique that is supposed to be faster than bloom filters. Find it online and try to use it.
Bonus 5: Check and see which technique is the fastest for your data. You may find libraries like timeit useful.

Connecting to a Cluster

This part is optional. If you don't have access to a cluster, skip on to the next section.

Many different companies offer Spark clusters with notebooks. The ones where Holden has worked are Google Cloud, Snowflake, Amazon AWS, Microsoft Azure, IBM Cloud, and Databricks. There are instructions on how to set up a cloud account at http://www.distributedcomputing4kids.com/cloud_setup/ . The instructions change a bit between companies.

Warning to helpers: Clusters cost money, even small ones can have real impact on your credit card bill and large ones can show up for department end of quarter budgets! Be careful to work within your budget and turn off the cluster when your kids (or executives) are finished. Some providers will offer a free credit. Be careful, though, because some will charge you once you go over the limit.

Once you have your cluster set-up you will need to install the Instagram library we installed before. Installing a library on a cluster can be complicated, depending on the cluster. Your helper should check this guide on how to install the package on the computers in your cluster.

If this is difficult for your helper, please tell them not to feel bad. People whose job it is to work with these clusters can sometimes spend hours getting them set up. Some providers make this easier than others, though.

Where to Go From Here!

I'm so glad you want to keep exploring! Distributed systems are fun and exciting. People in their jobs and at universities are trying to figure out how to build better ones. Many of these are open source systems, which allow contributions from others. Maybe when you have more experience, you can help us improve Apache Spark.

If you want to learn more about Apache Spark, there are many options. I've co-written a few books (Learning Spark and High Performance Spark, including a 2nd edition) that assume you have a lot of experience. Spark: The Definitive Guide and Learning PySpark are books by some of my friends that also assume a lot of experience. Unfortunately, there aren't any other books, yet, that do not assume experience.

If you want to learn Python, the programming language we used in this book, I'd recommend digging into Hour of Python. If books are your thing, Python Crash Course by Eric Matthes and Head First Python by Paul Barry are good options. The Head First series also has a Head First Learn How To Code by Eric Freeman, which uses Python. There are also many YouTube videos on how to get started with Python.

LIBRARY

You can try more exercises to help you explore:

- Weight the tags by the number of likes the photo received
- Only count tag use once per account. This way, if one of your friends tags every photo with #muffin but none of your other friends do #muffin won't show up in your list of popular tags.
- Rewrite your imports to just get the parts you need (e.g. from X import Y).
- Limit the tags you count to ones that were posted in just the last week. This is a lot of work since dates are tricky with computers, and the basic_instagram_library doesn't understand dates yet.
- Compute the average number of letters in the popular hashtags from your friends posts.

If collecting data from Instagram is boring to you and you don't have enough of your own data, try searching online. There are excellent public data sets about everything from taxi-cab rides, to movie watching, to weather. Many cities also have open data, including San Francisco.

I have a YouTube channel where I explore how open source software like Apache Spark is developed: https://www.youtube.com/user/holdenkarau. I do occasionally use impolite language so check with a parent / guardian or board member before watching.

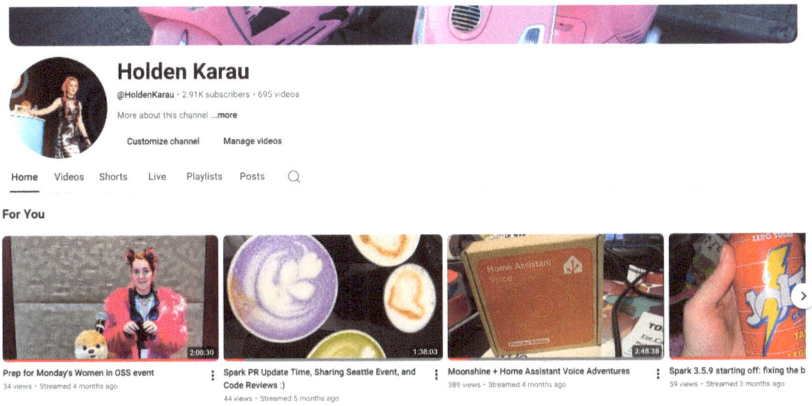

Here are some ideas of exercises you can do that will work well on local mode:

- Suggest bad flights by finding the airports which are furthest away from each other
- You can use Openflights data and the GeoPy library (or some math with radians)
- Find the most popular final obstacles on American Ninja Warrior.
- See if YouTube votes on previews predict movie reviews.
- Use the Movielens data & learn about Python web scraping.
- Find popular items on Cragistlist
- Find out if there is a relationship between the number of police calls and how safe a restaurant's food is if your city publishes these datasets
- Find the highest rated books by people who like the same books as you
- Use the Goodbooks-10k dataset. You can learn about "collaborative filtering."
- Calculate the weight of all the Pokemon you've ever caught
- Find your ideal Pokemon using https://www.kaggle.com/rounakbanik/pokemon and their total attack power https://www.kaggle.com/abcsds/pokemon

- Find what kind of Lego sets you can build with your parts
    - If you're just interested in building some cool Lego designs you can check out https://rebrickable.com/
    - Use the https://www.kaggle.com/rtatman/lego-database#sets.csv data to do it yourself.

Here are some ideas of exercises you can do that will probably require a cluster:

- Find popular items on ebay.
- Find the most mentioned pop stars on twitter.
- Look for "lost" "money" on the Blockchain (wallets that have not been used).
- Find differences in the news of successful companies and bankrupt companies
- Find where lightning does strike twice

If you enjoyed learning about Apache Spark in this format, and are over 13 you can sign up at http://www.distributedcomputing4kids.com/ to find more books on distributed computing and resources as they become available (if you're more on the kids side of kids and executives ask an adult).

I hope this has raised your interest in programming. It would be awesome if you joined the software industry. If you choose another path, that's totally OK too. Also, don't feel like you need only one path. I've gone back and forth on what I want to do over the years. Either way, having a fundamental understanding of programming/computers will benefit you. Also, programming is similar to solving puzzles and can be fun, especially when done with others. Wherever your adventures lead you, good luck, and have fun when you can.

Timbit (Holden's Dog) is proud of you for reading this far!

www.ingramcontent.com/pod-product-compliance
Lightning Source LLC
Chambersburg PA
CBHW041308210926
51847CB00005B/54
* 9 7 8 1 9 6 0 5 9 5 0 0 3 *